Original title:

Radiant Union

Author: Olivia Oja

ISBN HARDBACK: 978-1-80560-008-4

ISBN PAPERBACK: 978-1-80560-473-0

The Dance of Light and Love

In twilight's embrace, shadows play,
Two hearts entwined, they sway and stay.
Whispers of warmth, a gentle call,
In the realm of dreams, love conquers all.

Underneath the stars, a secret shared,
Every glance speaks, no need to be bared.
The moonlight guides, a soft lullaby,
In this dance of light, together we fly.

Illuminated Paths

Beneath the boughs, where silence dwells,
Footsteps softly tell their tales.
Each curve of earth, a story steeped,
In nature's arms, sweet secrets keep.

Lanterns aglow, with wisdom bright,
We traverse the path, hand in hand, light.
Every step leads, a call to roam,
In the heart's compass, always home.

A Symphony of Souls

Voices meld into a sacred blend,
Harmonies birthed, no need to pretend.
Each note a heartbeat, lost and found,
In this symphony, love's sweet sound.

Strings that resonate, dreams take flight,
In the orchestra's embrace, pure delight.
Every soul sings, a melody sweet,
Together we rise, joy's heartbeat.

Glimmers of Together

In fleeting moments, glimmers shine,
Together we weave, stories divine.
Through laughter and tears, we blaze a trail,
Bound by the warmth, our hearts unveil.

Flickers of joy, in the shared gaze,
Echoes of love, in a soft haze.
These precious seconds, forever they bind,
In the tapestry of us, solace we find.

Constellation of Hearts

In the night sky, we find our way,
Stars like whispers, softly sway.
Twinkling dreams in dark's embrace,
Each heartbeat shares a timeless space.

Guided by light, our spirits soar,
Together, we seek forevermore.
Across the velvet, we draw near,
A dance of souls, no hint of fear.

Constellations weave our stories bright,
In each twinkle, love takes flight.
Every pulse, a brighter spark,
In endless realms, we leave our mark.

Through galaxies, we share our flame,
Infinite journeys, never the same.
Hearts aligned, we navigate,
The cosmic fate we cultivate.

As we shine in the pale moonlight,
Every glance ignites the night.
In this vastness, we each play a part,
Connected forever, constellation of heart.

United in Brilliance

Together we stand, side by side,
In a world where stars collide.
Each flicker tells our tale anew,
United in brilliance, me and you.

With every glance, the skies ignite,
A dance of shadows, pure delight.
The universe hums a secret song,
In its rhythm, we feel we belong.

Woven in stardust, our dreams intertwine,
Glowing with love, forever divine.
In a tapestry of cosmic delight,
We shine together, a beautiful sight.

Bonded by fate, we dare to explore,
On this path, we long for more.
Through nebulae, we chase with glee,
Illuminated paths where our hearts roam free.

In the twilight, our hopes arise,
Together we'll chase the endless skies.
Guided by light, and love's embrace,
In brilliance united, we find our place.

Luminous Embrace

In twilight's tender glow, we find,
A warmth that wraps the heart and mind.
Each whisper soft, a gentle trace,
Into the night, a luminous embrace.

Stars align in tranquil skies,
Reflecting dreams and whispered sighs.
Together forged in night's sweet grace,
We share our lives in a radiant space.

The moon, our guide, in silver beams,
Illuminates the path of dreams.
Within this light, our souls interlace,
Creating shadows, a luminous chase.

With every heartbeat, light renews,
Each moment bright, as love imbues.
In our embrace, no fears can face,
The beauty found in a luminous space.

So let us wander, hand in hand,
Through starlit nights and golden sand.
In every step, a sacred place,
Together bound in a luminous embrace.

Threads of Light

We weave our hopes, a tapestry,
With threads of light, in harmony.
Each color glows, a story spun,
In unity, our lives are one.

Through the fabric of the night,
We seek the dawn, a guiding light.
A gentle touch, a soft refinement,
Threads of light form our alignment.

As dawn breaks through the shadows' veil,
Our woven dreams begin to sail.
With every strand, our hearts embrace,
Connected deeply in this space.

In laughter shared and moments bright,
We find our strength in threads of light.
From dusk till dawn, we shall embrace,
The beauty of our woven grace.

Forever bound, our spirits lift,
In every thread, the greatest gift.
Together shine in time and place,
Entwined forever with threads of grace.

Celestial Harmony

In cosmic dance, the stars align,
Creating rhythms, pure and divine.
Each note and pulse a sacred hymn,
In celestial harmony, we begin.

Planets spin in timeless flow,
While galaxies in stillness glow.
In endless skies, our spirits race,
Unified in this vast space.

With every heartbeat, we are one,
In stellar light, our souls have spun.
An orchestra of dreams we chase,
Embracing all in time and grace.

Through nebulous clouds, we weave our way,
Transforming night into a new day.
In this embrace, we find our place,
In celestial harmony, we find grace.

So let the heavens sing their song,
As we journey, we belong.
Within this vast and endless space,
Together, we find celestial grace.

Illuminated Togetherness

In the glow of love, we stand tall,
With every heartbeat, we hear the call.
Illumined paths, our spirits bright,
In illuminated togetherness, we ignite.

Hand in hand, we tread the light,
Facing challenges, hearts take flight.
With kindness shared, we find our place,
Creating bonds of warm embrace.

The world may dim, but we'll remain,
Shining bright through joy and pain.
In every moment, a shared space,
Illuminated together, we find grace.

In laughter's echo and silence's song,
We gather strength, we feel belong.
In every tear and every trace,
Together we shine, a warm embrace.

So here we stand, come what may,
With love as guide, we'll find our way.
In this dance of life, let's embrace,
The beauty found in illuminated grace.

The Glow of Togetherness

In the warmth of shared laughter,
Hearts dance like flames,
Embracing the light we gather,
United, we break the chains.

Through trials and tribulations,
We shine through the night,
Hand in hand, we find our way,
Creating bonds of might.

Every moment, a treasure,
In the glow, we see,
Together, we write our story,
Of love and unity.

When shadows start to linger,
Our spirits intertwine,
Together we rise, we move,
In a dance so divine.

The glow is ever brightening,
A beacon, clear and true,
In the heart of togetherness,
There's nothing we can't do.

Shimmering Connection

Across the vast dimensions,
We forge a shimmering tie,
A connection that transcends,
Reaching far beyond the sky.

Every glance tells a story,
In silence, we converse,
In the depths of our knowing,
We break barriers, immerse.

Like stars aligned in harmony,
We twinkle side by side,
In this shimmering moment,
There's no need to hide.

With every heartbeat echoing,
We resonate as one,
In the tapestry of feeling,
Our energies are spun.

No distance can divide us,
In this bond we share,
Together, we shine ever bright,
In love's gentle air.

Bright Threads of Affinity

Woven threads of friendship,
Color our lives with glee,
In the fabric of connection,
Together, we are free.

Like rivers flow together,
Joining in a grand design,
Our hearts beat in rhythm,
A pulse that feels divine.

Each moment we create,
Forms a vibrant strand,
In this beautiful tapestry,
Together we will stand.

Through laughter and through sorrow,
These threads will never fray,
In the loom of our existence,
We're shining every day.

A masterpiece unfolding,
In affinity, we're found,
Bright threads of love and kindness,
Forever intertwined.

United in Brilliance

In the light of shared visions,
We soar across the skies,
Bound by dreams and passions,
We rise, and rise, and rise.

With every spark ignited,
Together, we ignite,
In brilliance, united,
Our spirits take to flight.

Each moment holds a promise,
In the warmth of your embrace,
In the depths of our unity,
We find our sacred space.

Through storms and gentle breezes,
We navigate the tide,
In harmony, we flourish,
With love as our guide.

With every step we take,
We're stronger, hand in hand,
In this journey of brilliance,
Together we will stand.

Gleaming Affinity

In twilight's glow, we weave
Threads of laughter, softly spun.
Hearts aligned, they gently cleave,
In this world, we are as one.

Stars above, our guiding light,
Whisper secrets through the night.
Hands entwined, we feel so right,
Together strong, forever bright.

Moments shared ignite a flame,
Burning softly, never tame.
In your smile, I feel the same,
Gleaming love, an endless game.

Paths entwined by fate's design,
Every heartbeat, pure and fine.
In your eyes, I see the shine,
An affinity, divine sign.

As time flows like a river wide,
In your warmth, I will abide.
Through the storms, we will glide,
In gleaming love, we take our ride.

Shining Ties

Beneath the moon, our shadows dance,
Echoes whisper, a fleeting chance.
Hearts connected in a trance,
In this moment, we advance.

Every glance sparks a new glow,
Binding threads that softly flow.
Through the dark, our colors show,
Shining ties that ebb and grow.

In the laughter, we find peace,
Moments shared that never cease.
In this bond, our joys increase,
Shining ties that bring release.

Through the trials, we stand tall,
In each stumble, we will not fall.
Side by side, we hear love's call,
Shining ties that conquer all.

In the dawn, our spirits rise,
Love ignited, a sweet surprise.
In your heart, my spirit lies,
Shining ties beneath the skies.

Incandescent Whispers

In the shadow, light does breathe,
Softly glowing, we may cleave.
Through the silence, truths we weave,
Incandescent whispers, we believe.

Every sigh a spark ignites,
Warming souls on chillier nights.
In your presence, all feels right,
Incandescent dreams in flight.

With each heartbeat, we connect,
Unspoken words, our hearts reflect.
In this flow, we feel the effect,
Incandescent whispers we protect.

In the stillness, voices blend,
Softest moments, hearts transcend.
Together strong, we will not bend,
Incandescent whispers, never end.

Through the dusk, our spirits soar,
Hand in hand, we seek for more.
In love's embrace, we gently pour,
Incandescent whispers, our core.

Unity in the Divine Light

In the quiet dawn, we stand,
Bound by grace, love's gentle hand.
Hearts united, softly planned,
Unity in the divine land.

Through the trials, we remain,
Every joy, a sweet refrain.
In our laughter, no more pain,
Unity in love's domain.

Whispers travel on the breeze,
In your arms, I find my ease.
Together, always aim to please,
Unity brings the heart's release.

In the moment, skies align,
Every heartbeat, pure design.
In your gaze, the stars will shine,
Unity in the divine sign.

As day fades to night's embrace,
We find solace in this space.
Together, history we trace,
Unity, love's endless grace.

Unified in Glow

In the quiet of the night,
Stars gather in delight,
Waves of warmth embrace the air,
Unified, we shed our care.

Hand in hand, we walk the line,
Every heartbeat feels divine,
Through the shadows, we will tread,
In this glow, our fears are shed.

Every whisper, every song,
In each other, we belong,
Shining bright, our spirits soar,
Unified forevermore.

With our laughter, we ignite,
A beacon in the darkest night,
Together, we can light the way,
In our hearts, the love will stay.

Underneath the moonlit skies,
Magic twinkles in our eyes,
Bound by dreams, we rise above,
In this unity, we find love.

The Spark of Together

In the stillness, we ignite,
Two souls dancing, pure delight,
With a spark that lights the night,
Together, we take flight.

Fingers brush, a gentle tease,
Moments shared that bring us ease,
All around, a vibrant glow,
In the warmth, our feelings flow.

Through the chaos, we create,
A haven, a shared fate,
In each heartbeat, love will grow,
With every breath, our voices glow.

Quiet whispers, laughter shared,
In this life, we've always cared,
Side by side, let's chart our course,
Fueled by love, our glowing force.

From the embers, flames will rise,
Kindled dreams beneath the skies,
In this moment, we are strong,
In this bond, we both belong.

Lightyears of Affection

Across the vast and starry sea,
Your love travels endlessly,
Lightyears stretch, yet hearts align,
Through the cosmos, love will shine.

In the silence, whispers soar,
Echoes of us, forevermore,
Boundless skies, our dreams take flight,
In each other, purest light.

With every star, a promise made,
In the dark, our fears will fade,
Galaxies dance, a timeless flow,
Through the night, our spirits glow.

Navigating through the night,
In this journey, hearts feel right,
Together, we embrace the call,
Lightyears strong, we'll never fall.

Though the distance may seem wide,
In your love, I'll always bide,
Infinite as the moon above,
Time stands still in our sweet love.

Gleaming Pathways

On gleaming paths, our feet will tread,
Through the light where dreams are fed,
Together, hand in hand we roam,
In this journey, we find home.

With every step, our spirits rise,
Chasing dawns, beneath bright skies,
In the glow, we chase the day,
On these paths, we'll find our way.

Moments spark like morning dew,
In the warmth, it's me and you,
Side by side, no shadows cast,
In this bond, we'll hold steadfast.

Every turn, a new surprise,
In your gaze, the world complies,
Guided by our hearts' embrace,
On gleaming paths, we'll find our place.

Through the trials and the grace,
In your smile, I see my space,
Together, we will face the dawn,
Gleaming pathways, love goes on.

Eternal Embrace

In shadows deep where whispers lie,
Hearts entwined beneath the sky.
Time stands still, a sacred space,
Two souls lost in an eternal embrace.

When morning breaks with gentle rays,
Love's soft touch in tender blaze.
In every sigh, a promise made,
Together walking, unafraid.

Through vibrant nights and starry skies,
United dreams and timeless ties.
Every heartbeat echoes clear,
In quiet moments, love draws near.

Though seasons change and shadows creep,
In memories held, our spirits leap.
Forever bound, through thick and thin,
In sweetest joys, where love begins.

So hand in hand, let's face it all,
In every rise, in every fall.
With every glance, the world retraced,
Together, we seek our eternal embrace.

Luminous Bonds

Within each heart, a light ignites,
A bond forged bright with starry nights.
In laughter shared, a dance of fate,
Luminous ties that resonate.

Through trials faced and joys untold,
These ties of love, they shine like gold.
With every step, our paths align,
In unity, our spirits shine.

Like rivers flow, entwining dreams,
Carving valleys, glistening streams.
In vibrant hues, our canvas spread,
Each stroke a word we've never said.

With open arms, we face the chance,
In every moment, a sacred dance.
The light we share, a guiding spark,
Illuminates the paths grown dark.

So let us cherish, hold it tight,
This luminous bond, our shared light.
In every glance, in every cheer,
Together, love, we persevere.

Harmony in the Light

In morning glow, our voices rise,
A symphony beneath the skies.
With every note, a story sung,
Harmony found where hearts are young.

Through whispered words and gentle grace,
In unity, we find our place.
With open hearts, we share a dream,
Together strong, a flowing stream.

The colors blend, a canvas vast,
In every present, future, past.
With every breath, a melody,
In harmony, we come to be.

As sunbeams dance on fields of gold,
Our laughter shared, a tale retold.
In every tear, in every fight,
We rise anew, in the purest light.

So let us sing, our voices paired,
In harmony, our hearts ensnared.
With every joy that we ignite,
Together always, in the light.

Celestial Convergence

When twilight falls, the skies unite,
Stars awaken, shimmering bright.
In cosmic dance, our paths align,
Celestial hopes in dreams entwined.

With every pulse of the moon's embrace,
We find our truth in this vast space.
Time stands still as galaxies spin,
A journey deep, where love begins.

In every heartbeat, a universe sings,
Infinite tales and boundless things.
As stardust swirls in gentle breeze,
We find our peace, our souls at ease.

Through constellations, we drift afar,
Guided softly by the evening star.
In this vastness, we stand as one,
Eternal hope when day is done.

So let us soar, with hearts aligned,
In celestial realms, our fates entwined.
As night unfolds in its soft decree,
In the cosmic dance, we find our free.

Shimmering Connections

In the twilight's gentle glow,
Whispers of dreams begin to flow.
Hearts intertwine like ancient trees,
Roots of joy carried by the breeze.

Laughter echoes through the night,
Stars weave tales of pure delight.
Bonds crafted in the softest light,
Guiding souls till morning bright.

Fingers touch, a spark ignites,
Colorful paths in wondrous sights.
Each glance shared, a story told,
In every moment, love unfolds.

Through storms and calm, we stand as one,
Bright connections 'neath the sun.
In our hearts, we trace the lines,
Of shimmering ties that intertwine.

The Dance of Dews

Morning breaks, the world awakes,
Dewdrops glisten on leaf and flake.
Each drop a dance, a tale to tell,
Nature's magic cast a spell.

In soft whispers, they unite,
Reflecting dreams in the morning light.
As petals bloom, the story grows,
The dance of dews, in silence flows.

A gentle breeze stirs them around,
In unity, they gather 'round.
Each droplet a shimmering sphere,
Capturing moments, precious, dear.

As the sun climbs high in the sky,
The dance persists, it won't say goodbye.
Together they twinkle, together they gleam,
In nature's embrace, a beautiful dream.

Bright Threads of Affection

A tapestry woven with care,
Threads of warmth, a love we share.
Each stitch a moment, a gentle seam,
Binding our hearts in a common dream.

Colors merge in the softest light,
Painting our story, bold and bright.
Through laughter and tears, we find our way,
Threads of affection, come what may.

In every fold, a memory lives,
Of cherished times that love forgives.
With every heartbeat, the patterns grow,
Bright threads of affection, forever flow.

Hand in hand, through life's design,
We'll weave more tales, our souls align.
In this fabric, we'll always stay,
Creating a bond that won't decay.

A Spectrum of Togetherness

In every shade, we find our place,
A spectrum woven with gentle grace.
Like rainbows bright in the morning dews,
Together we shine, together we choose.

From vibrant reds to softest blues,
Each hue reflects the love we muse.
In moments shared, we intertwine,
A palette rich in dreams divine.

Through trials faced and laughter shared,
We paint our journey, showing we cared.
An artist's touch in every twist,
A spectrum of love, too bright to resist.

Together we dance in colors bold,
Stories of warmth in hues untold.
In this canvas, side by side,
A spectrum of togetherness, our guide.

Shimmering Whirlwind

In the dance of leaves, they twirl,
Colors blending in a swirl.
Whispers carried on the breeze,
Nature's beauty, hearts at ease.

Stars above begin to gleam,
In the night, we share a dream.
Moonlight guides our every step,
In this realm, no secrets kept.

Waves that crash upon the shore,
Rushing tides we all adore.
With each grain of sand we find,
Memories of heart and mind.

Laughter echoes through the night,
Filled with joy, a pure delight.
In this whirlwind, we are free,
Boundless moments, you and me.

As the dawn breaks into light,
Our spirits soar, taking flight.
In this shimmering embrace,
Love forever, time and space.

Divine Light of Togetherness

In the warmth of morning sun,
Hearts unite, our souls are one.
Hand in hand on this sweet quest,
In each other, we are blessed.

With a laugh that fills the air,
Moments cherished, love and care.
Every step, a tale to weave,
In this truth, we do believe.

Stars align in perfect grace,
In your eyes, I find my place.
Together, we can brave the night,
Courage sparkles in our sight.

When the shadows start to fall,
We will rise to heed the call.
Guided by our shining light,
Together, we can take flight.

In this dance of shared delight,
Woven tightly, hearts ignite.
With each breath, we stand as one,
In this life, our journey's spun.

Glorious Intersections

Paths that cross, a fated chance,
In this moment, hearts will dance.
Time stands still, as eyes embrace,
In this world's most tender place.

Journeys woven, tales unfold,
Simple stories, yet so bold.
Every heartbeat, every sigh,
Links us gently, you and I.

Through the chaos, we will find,
Peace and solace, intertwined.
In the noise, we hear the song,
Melodies where we belong.

In the twilight's soft embrace,
Friendship blooms at every pace.
With each laughter, memories blend,
In this life, love has no end.

As the stars come out to play,
We will chase the night away.
In the colors of the dawn,
Glorious intersections drawn.

Fusion of Bright Spirits

In the depths of every dream,
Love's a spark, a vibrant beam.
Together we ignite the night,
With a flame that feels so right.

Through the trials, hand in hand,
Building castles in the sand.
With each wave that sweeps the shore,
We create, we search for more.

Hearts united, souls entwined,
In the darkness, light we find.
In the laughter that we share,
Fusion flows, a bond so rare.

In the gardens of our hearts,
Every bloom a brand new start.
With each petal, hope will rise,
Filling dreams that touch the skies.

As the universe aligns,
In our hearts, the love defines.
Fusion of our bright spirits soar,
Together, we are evermore.

The Glow of Friendship

In laughter and whispers, we share our truth,
With bonds strong and warm, that shine like youth.
Through valleys of doubt, we stand side by side,
A glow in the dark, our hearts open wide.

With each gentle word, our spirits entwine,
Together we flourish, our souls brightly shine.
In moments of silence, we feel the embrace,
A beacon of hope, in this sacred space.

Through storms and through trials, our light stays aglow,
In the depths of our hearts, our friendship will grow.
A treasure unmeasured, it knows not an end,
In the tapestry woven, you're my dearest friend.

So here's to the laughter, the memories we make,
In the glow of our friendship, we never will break.
For each step we take, in harmony's flight,
Together we bask, in love's pure delight.

Together We Illuminate

In the shadows of doubt, we find our way,
With whispers of trust, we light up the day.
Your laugh is the spark, in a world so wide,
Together we stand, with joy as our guide.

Like stars in the night, our spirits align,
A dance of bright flames, your heart close to mine.
In moments of stillness, our hopes gently soar,
Together, dear friend, we shine evermore.

Through trials and triumphs, our paths intertwine,
With courage and kindness, our souls brightly shine.
In laughter and dreams, we bravely explore,
Together we illuminate, forever, encore!

On this journey of life, may we bask in the glow,
With each step we take, let our love only grow.
Through the ebbs and flows, let our hearts stay true,
Together we shine, like the morning dew.

A Tapestry of Radiance

Threads of laughter, stitched with care,
In the fabric of life, our stories we share.
Each moment a color, so vibrant and bright,
In the tapestry woven, we craft our own light.

From the smallest of gestures, to grand displays,
We weave our own magic, in so many ways.
Through trials, we gather each shimmering piece,
In the fibers of friendship, our joy finds release.

As sunbeams break through, our hearts dance in time,
With every connection, our spirits do climb.
Together we flourish, as flowers in bloom,
In this tapestry forged from kindness and room.

May the colors stay vibrant, may the threads never fray,
In the warmth of our laughter, we'll find a new way.
Through the seasons of life, our story unfolds,
A tapestry of radiance, brighter than gold.

Merging Echoes of Light

In the stillness of night, our whispers collide,
Two hearts intertwined, in a radiant tide.
With each gentle heartbeat, our spirits ascend,
Merging echoes of light, we find a true friend.

Through valleys of shadows, we walk hand in hand,
With trust as our compass, together we stand.
In laughter and tears, we paint our own way,
Through storms and through sunshine, come what may.

As stars softly twinkle, our dreams take their flight,
In melodies shared, we simply feel right.
With hope as our lantern, we'll travel afar,
Merging echoes of light, like a guiding star.

So here's to the journeys, to the paths yet to tread,
With courage in our hearts, let our spirits be fed.
In the brightness we find, may our souls unite tight,
For in every heartbeat, we merge echoes of light.

The Glow of Kinship

In twilight's embrace, we gather near,
Laughter and stories, each one sincere.
With hearts intertwined, like vines we grow,
Together we shine, in the gentle glow.

Through trials we stand, hand in hand,
In shadows we find, a bond that's grand.
A warmth that surrounds, in joy and in strife,
The glow of kinship, the light of our life.

In moments of silence, we feel the thread,
Connecting our souls, where often we tread.
With whispers like breezes, we gently weave,
The tapestry of love, in which we believe.

In laughter we soar, in sorrow we mend,
A circle of trust that will never end.
Through seasons that change, our hearts will remain,
Bound by a flame, that will always sustain.

So here's to the bond, ever bright and true,
In the glow of kinship, I'll cherish you.
With each step we take, and each dream we dare,
Together we'll dance, in the love we share.

Transcendent Bond

In the quiet depths of a whispered thought,
A transcendent bond, so dearly sought.
Like stars in the night, our souls align,
In the vastness of love, you are forever mine.

Through storms we journey, we face the tide,
In every heartbeat, you are my guide.
With eyes wide open, we see the sight,
Of dreams intertwining, in purest light.

In laughter we sculpt, our moments divine,
Each shared heartbeat, a sacred sign.
Through valleys of doubt, we rise and climb,
Together we flourish, transcending time.

In silence we find, a language rare,
A bond unbroken, beyond compare.
In every embrace, eternity dreams,
As love flows like water, in shimmering streams.

So let our hearts sing, in vibrant hues,
For the transcendent bond, we chose to muse.
In every sunrise, and moonlit night,
Together we'll travel, in endless light.

Unified in Brilliance

Two minds like constellations, perfectly placed,
Unified in brilliance, our spirits embraced.
Like rivers that merge, our lives intertwine,
Together we spark, a vision divine.

With courage, we dance on this vibrant stage,
Turning each chapter, like ink on a page.
With laughter as music, and dreams taking flight,
Unified in brilliance, we light up the night.

In shadows we stand, unyielding and strong,
The melody of harmony, our hearts belong.
In moments of stillness, our spirits find grace,
In the dance of existence, we find our place.

Embracing the journey, with passion and zeal,
With every step taken, there's magic we feel.
Together we flourish, a tapestry spun,
Unified in brilliance, we shine like the sun.

So let the world witness our luminous glow,
In every adventure, together we grow.
With love as our guide, we'll embrace every chance,
Unified in brilliance, forever we'll dance.

Harmony's Radiance

In the symphony of life, we play our part,
Harmony's radiance flows from the heart.
With notes intertwining, a sweet serenade,
In every embrace, our fears start to fade.

Through valleys and peaks, our voices unite,
In the warmth of connection, we find our light.
With laughter as rhythm, and dreams as the score,
Harmony's radiance, forever we'll soar.

In moments of stillness, we feel the grace,
The beauty of kindness, a warm embrace.
With every shared glance, a language we speak,
In the harmony of love, it's hope we seek.

A melody rising, like dawn in the sky,
With hands joined together, we reach and we fly.
In the dance of existence, a vision so bright,
Harmony's radiance, igniting the night.

So let the world listen, as we join our song,
In the heart's gentle rhythm, where we all belong.
With love as our anthem, together we sing,
In harmony's radiance, our spirits take wing.

Fusion of Luminescence

In the quiet night, light emerges,
Colors dance in the starry skies,
A blend of dreams in gentle surges,
Whispers of hope in the world's sighs.

Radiant hues in twilight's grasp,
Nature's heartbeat feels so near,
Moonbeams illuminate, shadows clasp,
The canvas of night, crystal clear.

Each flicker tells a hidden tale,
Of journeys taken, paths not crossed,
Through cosmic winds, we set our sail,
In unity, no brightness lost.

Sparkling gems in the velvet deep,
Hold secrets of ages yet untold,
In every twinkle, our spirits leap,
A tapestry of beauty, bold.

Together we rise, hand in hand,
Connected by the light we share,
In this fusion, we make our stand,
The universe breathes, bright and rare.

Stars Align in Harmony

In the vast expanse, stars collide,
Celestial bodies in sync they glow,
Guiding the wanderers with pride,
Their light a symphony in tow.

Each constellation a story spun,
Mapping the dreams of those who seek,
When night falls and the day is done,
In silent wisdom, the heavens speak.

Galaxies twirl in cosmic dance,
Creating magic, weaving fate,
Every shimmer a fleeting chance,
To find a love that feels so great.

Where wishes float on comet trails,
And hopes ignite in midnight's breath,
The night sky holds the grandest tales,
Whispered softly in love and death.

As the universe opens wide,
Our souls unite in astral flight,
Together we move, side by side,
In harmony, we face the night.

Twinkling Threads

Weaving light through the fabric of time,
Threads of silver in the dusky air,
Every twinkle a reason to rhyme,
A collage of moments we share.

Glimmers shining from hopes anew,
Casting shadows on paths ahead,
In each star, a promise so true,
A tapestry where dreams are fed.

Softly sparkles in the midnight hush,
Breath of the universe in our ears,
Through the silence, a gentle rush,
Of whispered secrets, hopes, and fears.

Entangled in this cosmic flight,
With hearts ablaze and spirits free,
We gather warmth from the starlight,
And weave our story through eternity.

In twinkling threads, our fate entwined,
A luminous map of love and grace,
Each moment cherished, forever aligned,
In the cosmos, we find our place.

Love's Brilliant Display

In the garden where fireflies dance,
Love ignites in a radiant glow,
Every heartbeat, a sweet romance,
As the night all around us flows.

A burst of colors in twilight's embrace,
Soft petals whispering secrets dear,
In each glance, a glow we chase,
Creating memories year by year.

With the moon as our shining guide,
We paint the world with dreams alive,
In every moment, we coincide,
Together, we flourish and thrive.

Like constellations that light the night,
Our bond glimmers in the dark,
With passion's spark, we take our flight,
In love's embrace, we leave our mark.

In the heavens, our hearts entwine,
A brilliant display so rare and bold,
With every shimmer, you are mine,
A story of love, forever told.

A Symphony of Light

In shadows cast by waning dusk,
Stars awaken, bright and husk.
Notes of silver ripple wide,
In this night, where dreams abide.

Whispers glide on gentle air,
Hope alights, a fleeting flare.
Moonbeams dance through open skies,
A symphony that never dies.

Harmony of every hue,
Painting skies with shades anew.
Silent echoes twirl and weave,
In this moment, we believe.

Each heartbeat sings, a tune so sweet,
In this serenade, we meet.
Spirits rise with every sound,
In this light, our souls are found.

Together woven, hearts take flight,
A tapestry of love and light.
Underneath the starlit dome,
In this symphony, we are home.

Embracing the Glow

Softly shines the morning sun,
Awakening, the day's begun.
Golden rays through trees they spill,
Nature's warmth, a gentle thrill.

Whispers linger on the breeze,
Beneath the shade of ancient trees.
Hands entwined, we walk the path,
Sharing laughter, joy, and wrath.

Every moment, bright and true,
In your gaze, I find the clue.
Hearts aglow, our spirits free,
In this glow, just you and me.

Evening falls, the sky ignites,
With colors bright, the world ignites.
In every hue, we find our way,
Embracing love, come what may.

Together we shall shine so bright,
In every shadow, share the light.
Hand in hand, through storm and show,
Forever in this love, we grow.

The Warmth of Together

Fires crackle, warmth draws near,
Laughter dances, hearts sincere.
With you close, the world seems right,
In our haven, love ignites.

Stories shared in whispered tones,
Building dreams, our sacred bones.
Eyes alight with shared delight,
In your arms, the long cold night.

Through the storms and through the strife,
Together, we embrace this life.
Each heartbeat close, a steady drum,
In this warmth, we all become.

Moments fleeting, but love endures,
In each hug, the heart ensures.
Together standing, side by side,
In this warmth, we shall abide.

As seasons shift and years unfold,
Hand in hand, our love's retold.
In the tapestry that we weave,
In this warmth, we still believe.

Elysium's Embrace

In Elysium, where dreams converge,
A sacred bond, our souls emerge.
Whispers carried on the breeze,
In this place, our hearts find ease.

Mountains rise, in vibrant glow,
Where love ignites and rivers flow.
Stars above like diamonds tossed,
In this valley, never lost.

Through the fields of endless bloom,
We wander free, dismissing gloom.
Every step, a dance of grace,
In this Eden, we find our place.

Hand in hand, the world feels right,
Bathed in dreams and soft moonlight.
Time stands still, as if to tease,
In Elysium, our hearts appease.

Here, forever, let us stay,
In love's embrace, we'll find our way.
In this paradise, so divine,
Together, always, your heart in mine.

When Stars Align

In the night sky, a dance unfolds,
With whispers carried through air so cold.
The spark ignites, a glimmering sign,
Moments like these, when stars align.

Hearts intertwine under a moon's embrace,
Time stands still in this sacred space.
Wishes are cast on celestial vines,
Lost in the dream where starlight twines.

The universe hums a sweet serenade,
And together we craft the dreams we've made.
Every heartbeat in perfect design,
A cosmic rhythm, when stars align.

As constellations weave tales from afar,
Guiding our paths like a shining star.
In each gentle pulse, our hopes combine,
The timeless magic when stars align.

Like notes in a symphony, pure and divine,
Together we flourish, your heart next to mine.
In the tapestry woven, fate's threads entwine,
A love everlasting when stars align.

Enchanted Kinship

Underneath the ancient trees,
Where laughter mingles with the breeze.
Friendship blooms in every heart,
A bond unbroken, never to part.

In secret groves, our stories unfold,
Wrapped in warmth, like tales retold.
With every glance, a knowing sign,
In this enchanted kinship, we shine.

Through sunlit glades and shadowed nooks,
We share our dreams, our favorite books.
Each moment cherished, a treasure divine,
An everlasting echo in time's design.

Side by side, we brave the storm,
Embracing all, in love we transform.
Together we dance, our spirits entwine,
In the heart's garden, a kinship divine.

Whispers and secrets that only we know,
A bond so strong, it continues to grow.
With laughter and courage, our paths align,
In this enchanted kinship, forever we shine.

The Flame of Companionship

In the quiet night, a fire glows bright,
Casting shadows, dancing with light.
We gather close, hearts filled with cheer,
The flame of companionship, always near.

Through laughter shared and stories spun,
Warmth ignites, two souls as one.
In the glow of embers, our spirits combine,
A bond unyielding, the flame divine.

Together we face the trials of fate,
Holding each other, never too late.
Through tempests and trials, our love will refine,
An unbreakable bond, this flame we define.

In the stillness of night, when the world leans close,
We find our rhythm, a love we can boast.
With every heartbeat, our souls intertwine,
Fueling the fire, this love so divine.

As the years pass by, we nurture the light,
With passion and kindness, our futures are bright.
In the warmth of our hearts, let our spirits align,
For in the embrace of companionship, we shine.

Whispers in the Glow

In the twilight hour, whispers arise,
Secrets woven beneath starlit skies.
With gentle caresses, the night comes alive,
In the soft amber glow, our dreams will thrive.

Through every shadow, our laughter spills,
Painting the night with joy that fills.
In your gaze, I find solace and flow,
Together we wander, where whispers grow.

With every heartbeat, the world fades away,
Captured in moments, forever we stay.
In the quiet hum of the night, we bestow,
A bond that transcends, where feelings glow.

As the stars weave tales from days of old,
In your arms, I feel ever bold.
With the flickering light, our spirits bestow,
An eternal dance where love's whispers grow.

So let us linger in this sacred embrace,
Time stands still in our timeless space.
In whispers and dreams, our hearts will flow,
Together forever, in love's gentle glow.

Glorious Convergence

In the twilight's gentle glow,
Two paths meet, hearts aglow.
Whispers dance on the breeze,
Promises carried through the trees.

Together we stand, side by side,
In this moment, we won't hide.
The world around us fades away,
In the magic of this day.

Fingers entwined, a sacred bond,
In each other's gaze, we respond.
The universe sings a sweet song,
In this convergence, we belong.

Colors swirl in the evening light,
Painting dreams that take flight.
Every heartbeat, a testament,
To the love that we represent.

As stars emerge, a wondrous sight,
Guiding us through the night.
In this dance of fate we find,
A glorious union, intertwined.

Lightwoven Hearts

In the dusk where shadows play,
Light weaves stories of the day.
Hearts alight with vibrant dreams,
Flowing softly like moonbeams.

Every glance ignites a spark,
Illuminating paths through the dark.
With laughter that rings like chimes,
Together we conquer space and time.

Echoes of joy in the air,
Every moment laid bare.
Two souls uniting, bright and free,
Crafting a lightwoven tapestry.

As dawn approaches, shadows fade,
The tapestry of love we've made.
In the warmth of the sun's embrace,
We find our forever place.

With every heartbeat, we ignite,
A radiant dance in pure delight.
Hand in hand, we'll journey far,
Guided by our shining star.

Brilliance Intertwined

Stars collide in the velvet sky,
In their glow, dreams learn to fly.
Each flicker tells a tale of old,
Of love and light, brave and bold.

From dusk till dawn, we'll explore,
A universe of whispers and lore.
Interlaced in the cosmic thread,
A dance of colors, softly spread.

In every heartbeat, a promise made,
In the silence, love won't fade.
Together we shine, a brilliant design,
In the fabric of fate, perfectly aligned.

With every challenge, we will stand,
Facing the storms, hand in hand.
For in the struggle, our strength is found,
With brilliance entwined, we are bound.

The galaxies swirl in our embrace,
In this tapestry, we've found our place.
As constellations write our name,
Together we burn in love's sweet flame.

The Harmony of Stars

Beneath a sky of velvet blue,
A symphony in silence grew.
Stars whisper secrets, bright and clear,
Drawing our souls ever near.

Each twinkle a note in the night,
Creating a melody of pure light.
Together we dance in cosmic bliss,
In the harmony that we can't miss.

With every heartbeat, time expands,
Together we shape these golden strands.
In the orchestra of moonlit dreams,
We find joy in the smallest themes.

The universe sways in gentle grace,
As we lose ourselves in this embrace.
Every glance, a sweet refrain,
Binding us in love's rich chain.

For as the stars begin to fade,
In this harmony, our hearts are laid.
Together we shine, a timeless spark,
Singing our song in the deep, dark.

A Symphony of Shimmer

In twilight's tender embrace,
Whispers of dreams take their flight.
Stars twinkle like lovers' grace,
Guiding the heart through the night.

Dancing shadows softly play,
Notes of a song unconfined.
Each shimmered moment will stay,
Eternally etched in the mind.

The breeze hums a gentle tune,
Crickets join in with delight.
Under the watchful moon,
We bask in the warmth of the light.

With every heartbeat, we find,
Melodies weaving through space.
A symphony of the kind,
That time cannot erase.

So let us cherish the night,
Where shimmer and dreams collide.
In the canvas of soft light,
Together, we'll take this ride.

The Light We Share

In a world of shadowed doubt,
Your smile ignites the flame.
In silence, our voices shout,
Bound by the same sweet name.

Through the storms that life may bring,
A beacon shining so bright.
Together, we laugh and sing,
Illumined by our shared light.

Step by step, we will go,
Hand in hand, hearts in sync.
In the dance of stars aglow,
We find the love that we think.

Like fireflies in the dark,
Creating magic in the air.
In every moment, a spark,
That tells of the light we share.

So here's to every sigh,
Every whisper, every stare.
As long as you are nearby,
We'll shine in the light we share.

Together Under Starlight

Beneath the expanse of night,
Where silence softly glows,
We find our hearts taking flight,
In the shimmer of the shows.

Hand in hand, we drift along,
The cosmos sings our song.
In this tapestry so strong,
We finally feel we belong.

Each star a promise of dreams,
Scattered across the skies.
Whispers of hope in moonbeams,
In our gaze, love never dies.

Together, with eyes wide open,
We paint our futures bright.
In this moment, unbroken,
We are home, heart's delight.

So let the world fade away,
In the stillness, we dare.
Together, come what may,
We'll shine, under starlight fair.

Illuminated Souls

In the depths where shadows lie,
Two souls begin to glow.
Through every laugh and sigh,
A radiant warmth we know.

Our spirits dance in the fire,
A light that cannot fade.
With every shared desire,
In your presence, I am made.

With countless stars in our gaze,
We chase the dreams that rise.
In the magic of our days,
The world reflects our skies.

Open hearts with no pretense,
Love's journey sets us free.
In a universe immense,
We create our own decree.

So let us wander as one,
With every heartbeat's roll.
Illuminated by the sun,
Forever, illuminated souls.

The Canvas of Light

On mornings bright, the stars awake,
With colors drawn, the dawn will break.
A canvas wide, where shadows fade,
Brushed in gold, the world remade.

The sun spills warmth on fields of green,
In every hue, a sight serene.
With every stroke, the heart finds peace,
In nature's art, all worries cease.

The sky, a palette of dreams untold,
With whispers soft, the air is gold.
As light cascades on river bends,
A dance of shadows, where time mends.

Each day unfolds a tale of grace,
In every glance, a warm embrace.
With every beam, the soul takes flight,
In the endless beauty, hearts ignite.

This canvas vast, forever bright,
A masterpiece of pure delight.
In the quiet moments, we find our way,
In the canvas of light, we choose to stay.

Seeking Celestial Bonds

Underneath the endless skies,
We search for truths in ancient skies.
With whispers soft, the stars align,
In cosmic dance, our souls entwine.

A journey deep through night's embrace,
We trace the paths, we find our place.
With every breath, the universe sings,
In harmony, our spirit rings.

From distant worlds, the echoes call,
In every heartbeat, we feel them all.
With each new twinkle, hope ignites,
A guide through dark, the stars are lights.

We walk the earth, yet reach for more,
As dreams ignite, our spirits soar.
In every glance, a spark of fate,
In celestial bonds, we resonate.

As night unfolds its magic rare,
We find our peace, our hearts laid bare.
In endless skies, we seek and find,
The ties of stars that bind mankind.

The Glimmering Path

Through misty woods, where shadows play,
A glimmering path leads me away.
With every step, the light will guide,
In nature's arms, I can abide.

Soft whispers weave through ancient trees,
Where sunlight dances with the breeze.
The golden rays in emerald glow,
Reveal the way, as spirits flow.

Upon this trail, my heart takes flight,
With every twist, the world feels right.
In fleeting moments, magic blooms,
As flowers whisper in sweet perfumes.

The glimmering path, a sacred thread,
With visions bright, my spirit's fed.
In every turn, new wonders greet,
In nature's touch, my soul's complete.

As twilight falls, the stars are near,
A guiding light, both bright and clear.
In every step, I feel the truth,
On this glimmering path, I find my youth.

A Voyage of Light

Setting sail on waves of glow,
With every breath, the currents flow.
In twilight's arms, the stars ignite,
A voyage bold, a dance of light.

With sails unfurled, we chase the dreams,
Through silken skies and silver streams.
Each moment drips like honey sweet,
As time reveals its rhythmic beat.

The ocean sings a song of peace,
Where all worries find their release.
In every wave, our hopes arise,
A tapestry beneath the skies.

As dawn breaks forth with golden rays,
We write our tales in morning haze.
With every pulse of nature's heart,
Our journey leaves its timeless mark.

In the radiance of day's embrace,
We forge ahead, we find our place.
On this voyage bright, we sail through night,
In a world alive, we chase the light.

Eclipsed by Togetherness

In shadows cast where hearts align,
Two souls entwined, a bond so fine.
The world may fade, yet we remain,
Together strong, we bear the strain.

A whispered laugh, a gentle sigh,
In silent nights, our dreams will fly.
With every tear, we learn to grow,
In love's embrace, we'll face the woe.

The stars may dim, the moon may wane,
But in your light, I've found my gain.
Through storms we dance, through pain we sing,
In togetherness, our hearts take wing.

With every step, we share the load,
On this tough path, you've eased the road.
A bond like ours, strong yet so sweet,
In love's sweet symphony, we meet.

So if the world should cast its doubt,
In unity, we stand throughout.
For in the dark, our light will shine,
Eclipsed by love, forever divine.

The Bright Side of Us

Amidst the clouds, your smile breaks through,
A beacon bright, in skies so blue.
In every glance, a spark ignites,
Together we weave our endless nights.

The sun will set, the stars will gaze,
But in your warmth, I find my daze.
We chase the dawn, hand in hand,
In every moment, together we stand.

Through whispers soft, and laughter loud,
You lift my spirit, you make me proud.
In every step, we find our way,
A brighter path, where dreams can play.

With eyes like fire, we'll light the dark,
In this vast world, you are my spark.
A story written, just for two,
In the bright side of us, love stays true.

As days unfold, and seasons change,
Our bond will grow, it won't feel strange.
Together we shine, through thick and thin,
In the journey of love, we both will win.

Tapestry of Warmth

In woven threads of gold and red,
Our stories blend, where love is bred.
A tapestry made of shared delight,
Each moment stitched, in soft moonlight.

The warmth of home, where hearts convene,
In laughter's echo, our souls have seen.
With every hug, the world feels right,
In our embrace, we chase the night.

The gentle hum of life's sweet song,
In every breath, where we belong.
In this rich fabric, strong and true,
A bond that's formed, just me and you.

With colors bright, and patterns bold,
Our love's the thread that can't be sold.
Through time's embrace, we'll weave anew,
In this tapestry, just me and you.

As seasons pass, and years may align,
Our story unfolds, a design divine.
Hand in hand, we'll journey afar,
In the tapestry of warmth, you are my star.

Celestial Circle of Light

In the night sky, our dreams take flight,
Through cosmic dance, in endless night.
Two hearts united, shining so bright,
In this celestial circle of light.

With every heartbeat, the stars align,
Your hand in mine, a love so fine.
We draw our hopes from the universe,
In constellations, we'll script our verse.

Through galaxies, our spirits roam,
In your embrace, I feel at home.
The moonlit glow, a path we trace,
In this circle, we find our place.

When shadows linger, and clouds appear,
In this light, we conquer fear.
Together we shine, against the night,
In this celestial circle of light.

As time unfolds, and dreams take flight,
Forever bound, in love's pure rite.
Together we journey, with hearts alight,
In this sacred circle, we find our might.

The Chorus of Joy

In laughter's sweet embrace, we find,
A melody that lifts the mind.
With every heartbeat, joy does grow,
In this chorus, let love flow.

Through dancing skies and sunlit days,
We weave together, find our ways.
Each moment shared, a treasure bright,
In the chorus, hearts take flight.

With open arms, we greet the morn,
In unity, our souls reborn.
A symphony of hopes and dreams,
In joyous echoes, love redeems.

As seasons change, this song remains,
In sunshine's warmth and gentle rains.
Together, strong, we rise above,
Our chorus sings, a song of love.

So let the world hear our refrain,
A dance of joy, a sweet campaign.
With voices raised, united, free,
In harmony, we'll always be.

Haloed Hearts

In twilight's glow, we softly meet,
Two haloed hearts, a rhythm sweet.
With every glance, the stars ignite,
In whispered dreams, we take our flight.

Your laughter echoes through the night,
A guiding star, a beacon bright.
With gentle hands, we touch the sky,
In haloed love, we learn to fly.

The moon witnesses our tender grace,
In every heartbeat, time and space.
Together woven, soul to soul,
In haloed light, we feel whole.

Through ups and downs, we stand so true,
With every step, we start anew.
In sacred bonds, our spirits soar,
With haloed hearts, we need no more.

So let the world see our embrace,
In cherished moments, we find our place.
With hands entwined, we face the stars,
In haloed love, forever ours.

Dazzling Connections

Like fireflies that dance at dusk,
Our spirits spark, creating trust.
In every glance, a world does bloom,
Dazzling connections, lighting the room.

Through laughter shared and stories told,
In every moment, memories unfold.
With gentle whispers, hearts can weave,
In dazzling bonds, we believe.

As seasons change, we find our way,
In colorful threads that never fray.
With open hearts, we paint the night,
Dazzling connections, pure delight.

Though life may throw its twists and turns,
In every lesson, a fire burns.
Together, strong, we face the tide,
In dazzling love, we confide.

So let us cherish what we share,
In every hug, a silent prayer.
With every heartbeat, ever true,
Dazzling connections, me and you.

Elysian Ties

In gardens where the blossoms sway,
Elysian ties light up the day.
With gentle touches, we align,
In sacred whispers, hearts entwine.

Through every storm, our roots grow deep,
In shared joys, our souls we keep.
With nature's song, we dance as one,
Elysian ties, forever spun.

In sunlight's glow and moonlit skies,
Our dreams take flight, our spirits rise.
With open heart, we face the dawn,
In elysian love, we are reborn.

So let life's canvas be our stage,
In every chapter, turn the page.
With laughter shared, your hand in mine,
Elysian ties, a love divine.

In fleeting time, we find our grace,
In endless moments, we embrace.
With every heartbeat, we aspire,
Elysian ties, our hearts' desire.

United in a Spectrum

In colors bright, we stand as one,
Together under the warming sun.
Each hue a thread in vibrant weave,
A tapestry of dreams we believe.

Through stormy nights, we hold the line,
In every shade, our souls entwine.
With every glance, a spark ignites,
In this vast world, we find our rights.

Each difference blooms like flower fair,
A spectrum wide, we boldly share.
Embracing contrast, hand in hand,
Our unity, a stronger strand.

From red to blue, the heartbeats sync,
In whispered words, we stop and think.
Together we rise, with voices clear,
In harmony, we conquer fear.

So let us dance in shades of praise,
United hearts set paths ablaze.
In every color, find the art,
Together vibrant, never apart.

The Light We Share

In quiet moments, two souls align,
Under starlit skies, your hand in mine.
With every laugh, a ray appears,
Illuminating paths through all our fears.

The glow between us softly burns,
A beacon bright, as each heart turns.
Together casting shadows away,
In light we trust, day after day.

Like sunflowers reaching for the sun,
In every challenge, we are one.
The warmth we share, a sweet embrace,
In every moment, find our place.

Through darkest nights, our fire glows,
With whispered dreams, our spirits rose.
In every spark, there's hope confined,
The light we share, forever binds.

So let us gather in the glow,
In every laugh, let love bestow.
With open hearts, the world will see,
The light we share sets our hearts free.

Bonds That Shine

In laughter's echo, hearts connect,
Invisible ties that we protect.
Through trials faced, we stand so tall,
In every stumble, we rise, we call.

Moments cherished in time's embrace,
A lasting bond no one can erase.
With every story shared in trust,
We build a fortress, strong and just.

In rainy days, under the gray,
We find the light that leads the way.
Each whispering word, a gentle guide,
In bonds that shine, we never hide.

Through winding paths where shadows play,
Our spirits shine, come what may.
In unity, our hearts define,
The beauty found in bonds that shine.

So let us celebrate this grace,
With every smile, a warm embrace.
Together we weave our stories fine,
This tapestry of bonds that shine.

Celestial Ties

In twinkling stars, our fates align,
Celestial whispers, forever entwined.
The moonlight dances on the sea,
Binding our hearts in harmony.

As comets soar across the night,
Our spirits lift, taking flight.
In every dream, the cosmos hears,
A symphony beyond our fears.

Through galaxies where rivers gleam,
In stardust trails, we find our dream.
Each shooting star a wish set free,
In cosmic dance, just you and me.

These ties of light—our guide divine,
In darkened skies, our souls combine.
With every heartbeat shared in time,
We forge our path, so proudly prime.

So let us journey, wander far,
Hand in hand beneath each star.
In the vast night sky, our spirits fly,
Connected by these celestial ties.

Luminous Journeys

With each step taken, shadows fade,
In the heart of night, our dreams invade.
Stars above whisper tales of old,
Guiding us onward, brave and bold.

Paths entwined in golden hues,
Winding through the nightly blues.
We chase the dawn, a new refrain,
In the warmth of light, we find our gain.

Moments fleeting, yet they shine,
In the tapestry of time divine.
Every heartbeat, a story told,
In luminous journeys, we break the mold.

Echoes linger in the air,
Memories glimmer, rare and fair.
Together we forge a brighter way,
In luminous travels, night turns to day.

So let us wander, hand in hand,
Through the gentle sweep of silver sand.
For in our hearts, the light will grow,
In luminous journeys, together we glow.

Threading Light's Embrace

In the quiet dusk, a whisper sighs,
Threads of light weave through the skies.
With gentle fingers, we pull the strands,
Creating dreams with tender hands.

Every glimmer paints the air,
Hope unfurling, light laid bare.
We dance in shadows, twirling free,
In the embrace of what will be.

As night deepens, colors blend,
Unity found, where journeys bend.
Each thread a story, strong and clear,
In threading light, we conquer fear.

Moments shimmer, bright and wise,
Weaving wishes, as time flies.
In this tapestry, we find our place,
In the warmth of light's embrace.

So let our spirits always rise,
In radiant patterns, we realize.
For in each stitch, love intertwines,
In threading light's embrace, our soul shines.

Shining Harmony

In every note, the silence breaks,
Melodies dance, the heart awakes.
Voices mingle in a sweet refrain,
Creating harmony, joy, and pain.

With gentle hands, we shape the sound,
Together, in echoes, we're unbound.
In this symphony, we find our way,
Shining brightly, come what may.

Notes entwine, like stars that gleam,
In the stillness, we chase the dream.
Each chord a heartbeat, strong and true,
In shining harmony, we start anew.

Let the music lift our souls,
In the rhythm, the spirit rolls.
With every harmony, we unite,
In the glow of love's pure light.

So sing with me, let voices soar,
In this shining harmony, we explore.
For through the music, we rise and blend,
In love and rhythm, we transcend.

The Luminous Ties That Bind

Through distant skies, our spirits link,
In the glow of stars, we softly think.
Invisible threads that pull us near,
The luminous ties, forever clear.

In laughter shared, we find our roots,
Among the shadows, love bears fruits.
Each memory sparkles like a star,
In the tapestry, we've come so far.

Through every storm, we stand as one,
In the light of dawn, our fears are gone.
Together we weave a tale unique,
The luminous ties forever speak.

With every heartbeat, our shadows dance,
In the light of love, we find our chance.
Together we rise, hand in hand,
In the luminous ties, we make our stand.

So let us cherish, let us hold tight,
In every moment, let love ignite.
For the ties that bind through all we face,
Are luminous threads of grace and space.

Illuminated Journeys

With lanterns bright, we set our course,
Through winding paths, we find our force.
Each step we take, a tale unfolds,
In shadows deep, our courage holds.

The night sky glimmers, a map so vast,
We chase our dreams, the die is cast.
With every heartbeat, a spark ignites,
Illuminated paths, our guiding lights.

In whispered winds, the secrets flow,
Our hearts entwined, together we grow.
Through thickets dense and mountains tall,
In unity we rise, we never fall.

The stars above, a promise clear,
In every struggle, we persevere.
With open hearts, we boldly roam,
In journeys shared, we find our home.

The sun will rise, as we believe,
In this adventure, we shall achieve.
Together, hand in hand, we go,
Illuminated journeys, forever glow.

The Delight of Togetherness

In laughter shared, our spirits soar,
The joy of being, we can't ignore.
With every smile, our hearts align,
In simple moments, love's design.

Through seasons bright, and storms that rage,
We write our story, page by page.
With tangled hands, we dance in rain,
In every heartbeat, we break the chain.

The warmth of hugs, a cozy embrace,
In shadows cast, we find our place.
With whispers soft, and dreams so vast,
The bond we share, forever will last.

In mundane days, we find the glow,
In every glance, our feelings show.
Together we face the world outside,
In all we do, love is our guide.

In quiet nights, as stars appear,
The delight of togetherness draws near.
With open hearts, and eyes that gleam,
In every moment, we live the dream.

Bright Horizon of Affection

Beneath the skies, our hearts take flight,
As shadows fade, we find our light.
With every dawn, new hopes arise,
In bright horizons, love never lies.

Through valleys low and mountains high,
We chase the sun, our spirits fly.
With every step, a promise made,
In each embrace, our fears allayed.

The warmth of love, a gentle fire,
In every heartbeat, we inspire.
With eyes that meet, our dreams align,
In this journey, your heart is mine.

Beyond the doubts, the dark, the gray,
Together we soar, come what may.
With every breath, our souls entwined,
In bright horizons, true love we find.

As sunsets fade, the stars ignite,
In every moment, pure delight.
With hope as guide, we walk the line,
In bright horizons, our spirits shine.

Chasing Sunlit Dreams

In fields of gold, where shadows dance,
We chase our dreams, take every chance.
With every step, the world unfolds,
In sunlit rays, our future molds.

With open arms, we greet the dawn,
In laughter shared, our fears are gone.
With every whisper, the magic grows,
In sunlit dreams, our true path flows.

We wander far, with hearts so free,
Through valleys wide, by land and sea.
With every sunrise, new hopes ignite,
In chasing dreams, our souls take flight.

As twilight falls, the stars will gleam,
In every heartbeat, we live the dream.
With woven paths, and hands held tight,
In chasing sunlit dreams, all feels right.

Together we rise, hand in hand,
In every moment, together we stand.
With eyes on horizons, our hearts will beam,
In chasing dreams, we weave our theme.

The Brilliance of Us

In the quiet of the night, we shine,
With laughter drawing stars, so divine.
Hand in hand, we chase the light,
Together we rise, hearts taking flight.

Moments flicker, like a flame,
Every glance, echoing your name.
In this bond, a radiant glow,
Two souls entwined, together we grow.

Whispers echo in the breeze,
Cradled softly among the trees.
A tapestry woven with care,
In every thread, our love laid bare.

Time dances, yet we stand still,
Together we climb every hill.
With each heartbeat, a new embrace,
In this brilliance, we find our place.

Bound by dreams, we light the way,
In shadows cast, we choose to stay.
The brilliance of us, bright and true,
A shining path, just me and you.

Dance of the Luminous

Underneath the moonlit sky,
Stars are twirling, oh so high.
In a rhythm only we know,
Our hearts beat soft, like whispers flow.

Every movement speaks of grace,
As we find our special space.
Hands entwined in gentle sway,
Lost in this luminous ballet.

The world fades a little more,
As we dance towards love's open door.
In each step, magic unfolds,
As our story of light is told.

With every twinkle, joy ignites,
In the warmth of endless nights.
With a spark that never tires,
We dance on dreams, stoking fires.

Together, we chase the dawn,
A dance of two, forever drawn.
In the glow of a shared delight,
We move as one, through the night.

Hearts Across Horizons

Across the waters, our hearts align,
Through every distance, love is a sign.
Mountains may rise, rivers may flow,
Yet together we grow, though far we go.

With every sunset, I feel you near,
In the whispers of winds, you appear.
No borders can hold what we share,
Our connection a light, vibrant and rare.

In dreams, I wander through your eyes,
Collecting stardust from midnight skies.
Each dawn brings us closer still,
With hope in our hearts, we find the will.

A bridge of dreams joins our souls,
In every heartbeat, love consoles.
Through valleys deep and skies so wide,
We walk this path, forever side by side.

So here I stand, arms open wide,
To meet you where the worlds collide.
Hearts across horizons, forever beat,
In a dance of love, perfectly sweet.

A Glow of Affinity

In the glow of the evening light,
We gather close, hearts feeling right.
A touch, a smile, a silent word,
In this moment, souls are stirred.

Like fireflies that flicker in the dark,
Your presence ignites a gentle spark.
With laughter echoing through the trees,
Together we sway with the rustling leaves.

Every secret shared, a thread interlaces,
In the fabric of time, we find our places.
A bond that ties in a warm embrace,
In the glow of affinity, we find our grace.

As seasons change, and years roll by,
We'll cherish each moment, you and I.
Through every storm that comes our way,
Our light will shine, come what may.

So here's to us, in joy and cheer,
In every heartbeat, I hold you near.
A glow that forever will stay,
In the dance of love, we'll find our way.

The Resplendent Chorus

In twilight's glow, we sing a song,
Of whispers soft, where hearts belong.
Each note a promise, pure and bright,
Together we dance, our souls take flight.

A symphony of joy we weave,
In every breath, we dare believe.
Beneath the stars, our laughter flows,
A tapestry of love that grows.

The echo of dreams, a vibrant thread,
With every heartbeat, joy widespread.
In harmony, we find our place,
The world aglow with love's embrace.

The moonlight bathes our sacred ground,
In every hug, connection found.
The melody lingers, sweet and clear,
In this resplendence, we have no fear.

With open hearts, we give and take,
Through every rise, through every quake.
In this chorus, we stand as one,
Together, we shine just like the sun.

Celestial Bonds of Affection

Within the stars, our spirits soar,
Guided by love, we seek for more.
Each heartbeat whispers, soft and true,
In cosmic realms, it leads to you.

Together we reach for skies divine,
In this vast space, our fates entwine.
A dance of light, we twirl and spin,
In every moment, love begins.

The constellations map our way,
In every night, we find our play.
With eyes aglow, we chase the dawn,
In this embrace, we are reborn.

The universe sings a timeless tune,
In every phase of the glowing moon.
Through trials fierce, our bonds hold tight,
In darkest times, we still find light.

Celestial paths that intertwine,
A bond unbroken, yours and mine.
In this affection, we find our grace,
A love that time cannot erase.

Dawn of Connection

As daylight breaks, our hearts align,
In golden hues, our souls entwine.
A tender gaze, a soft hello,
In every moment, love will grow.

Awakening dreams beneath the sun,
Each step together, we are one.
With open arms, we greet the morn,
In every laugh, a bond is born.

The world awakes, in colors bright,
With you beside me, all feels right.
In every sunrise, hope we see,
A journey shared, just you and me.

The whispers of dawn, a gentle chime,
In every second, love's sweet rhyme.
With each heartbeat, our spirits blend,
In this connection, there's no end.

With every breath, we hold so near,
In this new light, we cast out fear.
Together we walk, hand in hand,
In this dawn, our love will stand.

Glow of Companionship

As evening falls, our shadows play,
In gentle light, we find our way.
With laughter shared, our spirits soar,
In this companionship, we want for more.

Side by side, through thick and thin,
In every loss, we both will win.
The glow of love lights up the night,
With you, my world feels pure delight.

Through storms that rage, we'll stand our ground,
In every moment, our hearts are bound.
The warmth we share, a beacon bright,
In every dark, we bring the light.

With whispered dreams and secrets sweet,
In every challenge, we won't retreat.
Our hearts entwined like vines that grow,
In this embrace, we always know.

The years may pass, but love stays true,
In every glance, I see us two.
With steady hands, we'll build our way,
In glow of companionship, we'll stay.

www.ingramcontent.com/pod-product-compliance
Ingram Content Group UK Ltd.
Pitfield, Milton Keynes, MK11 3LW, UK
UKHW021301280125
4330UKWH00005B/83

9 781805 600084